Connection Points with God

John W. Matthews

by Zoey – epublishinghelp.com ISBN: 978-2-9217-1415-0

DEDICATION

Dedicated to our interfaith (retired) Monday Wisdom Group, who for five plus years has been meeting to discuss and assemble our collective understandings from a lifetime of making 'connection points' with the beyond, hoping to share our wisdom with the next generation.

Table of Contents

Foreword

In a time when nothing about religion seems stable or beyond question, a reflection that gets to the heart of the matter is most welcome. Virtually all religious communities, forms, rituals, doctrines, polities, ethics and actions are being contested. People are dropping out of organized religion in substantial numbers. Seekers are exploring alternatives of many kinds. Politics is invading and dividing the pews. Secularism seems to reign. What is the heart of the matter about religion anyway, one may wonder.

John Matthews has brought an extraordinary background and set of experiences to addressing just such a question. A decades-long career as a Lutheran pastor is a base upon which he has added significant scholarship and interfaith engagement. From a seminary student interest in Dietrich Bonhoeffer to later becoming president of the International Bonhoeffer Society-English Language Section and publishing two books about Bonhoeffer's spirituality, he has branched into Jewish-Christian relations and study of the Holocaust. He has expressed this interest and contributed at the level of crafting denominational theological position statements and, in his congregation, practicing observance of the Shoah as well as having rabbis preach during Sunday worship services.

As one chapter has led to another, including – for John – teaching college religion courses, he has reached out to initiate and deepen personal and professional relationships and work with Muslims and Native Americans. With such a rich range of relationships and experiences, his appreciation of the experiences of the 'other' has led him to what some might call deep 'appreciative inquiry' into his own and others' traditions. Others might call it something closer to radical questioning and exploration of what is at the very core of religion, namely, the various means by which humans experience connection with the divine/God. He helpfully categorizes these connections as places, events, people and writings. Leaning toward experience as the ultimate source and origin of religious authority, he pastorally and appreciatively explores how humans have invariably, necessarily and helpfully relied on theses specific means, and the forms they take in various traditions.

The radical, and very helpful, part of his exploration is tenderly and courageously exposing how any of the means humans rely on – aspects regarded as the most sacred items within their traditions' repertoire – can become overly regarded to the point of worship and idolatry. They then become ends rather than the human, relative, limited means they are in the face of the infinite mystery of the divine, that all religions point to, but cannot contain in any form.

Matthews' humility and courage show in his willingness to examine his own experience and tradition, of which he was a professional

John W. Matthews

advocate and practitioner throughout his career, asking: are we arrogantly raising our own means above others, in ways that result in negative 'otherizing,' while fooling ourselves that we have cornered a piece of the divine revelation that others haven't. Such a process has led him to make a case for healthy pluralism and respectful regard for others, an attitude that is far too often lacking in the religious landscape. I'm sure readers of different traditions will experience the invitation to deeper humility, appreciation and respect for their own and others' traditions, along with a pinch of confrontation with our own tendencies to arrogance and idolatry. Matthews provides a helpful and positive guide to the heart of the matter, our human potential for connection with the divine.

Rev. Dr. Tom Duke

Introduction

It has been my experience that most – not all – people seek in this life some 'points of connection' with the absolute, the divine, with God. Many people are introduced to the idea of a 'beyond' at a very early age; perhaps beginning with prayers at bedtime to grace offered at mealtime to religious class instruction, these young ones imbibe religion like their mother's milk. Still other people never experience religious family rituals, hence are not introduced to things like God, faith, prayer, worship and Heaven. Regardless of formal or informal introduction or indoctrination to things religious, most – not all – people do seem curious and inquire at some time during their life about that which lies beyond our world, above our ceilings and beneath life's surface, before our births and after our deaths. Being dependent on people and circumstances every day, in so many ways, folks often inquire about life's ultimate dependence; seeing all things around us as derived from something or someone, folks ask about an ultimate source from which we might come, life's derivation; as beings who most often seek purpose and meaning in life, folks wonder about an ultimate purpose and meaning. Again, not every person wonders about things beyond, but at some time or other such ultimate questions involving our dependence and derivation and purpose and meaning visit most human beings.

My curiosity regarding people's 'Connection Points' with the absolute, the divine, with God, is a result of several decades of being with people from many states, many countries, numerous cultures, and multiple religions, in short, a plethora of human beings, many of whom practice quite different religious faiths than me. When asked, these beautiful people can relate significantly different experiences of connection points with the beyond. Of course, my listening to these others is always shaped by the way that I have experienced connection points with the beyond. I am a textbook case of one who has transitioned through James W. Fowler's Stages of Faith (1981), maturing from Stage One (Intuitive-Projective) to Stage Two (Mythic – Literal) to Stage Three (Synthethic-Conventional) to Stage Four (Individuative-Reflective) to Stage Five (Conjunctive) to Stage Six (Universalizing Faith). At age seventy-five, and entering my final stage of life's journey, I find myself entering Fowler's Stage Six of religious growth (Universalizing Faith). While great numbers of people get stuck at one of the intermediate stages of religious growth (often stage three or four), it has been my good fortune to clumsily move through each stage, pausing, but not getting stuck. For this I am very grateful, and give credit to my family, my friends, my teachers, my parishioners, and my God.

Such an evolution of religious faith, such a maturation along life's journey, involves a recognition that "God is greater than both of us" (Rev. Richard Borgstrom, a colleague from Afton, Minnesota). My earlier, more arrogant, need to have a corner on the divine has morphed into a humble appreciation for the many ways the divine has connection with people. Somewhere between stages four and five (Fowler) comes an ever– expanding awareness that connection points with God happen in a variety of ways for people. While a person claiming to possess the one true connection point with God would appear to offer certainty and security, such a 'monopoly on salvation' usually becomes harder and harder for persons to maintain as they experience the wonderful wide world before us, a world populated with a marvelously diverse humanity. The chapters before you represent my attempt to describe: the human desire for connection with the beyond, some events that have provoked divine connection, some places where connection has happened, some people who have been regarded as intermediaries for connection with the beyond, some writings through which people have experienced authoritative wisdom from beyond, some dynamics and risks people experience when attempting to connect with the beyond in distorted ways, like perfectionism and idolatry, and finally the beauty of pluralism as something to celebrate – not resist – as a reward of recognizing many connection points with God beyond our own.

Chapter One

Human Desire for Connection with the Beyond

We will focus in the pages that follow on the human curiosity and experiences that prompt inquiry about something or someone beyond, acknowledging that some people have little or no desire to inquire about– or speak about – anything or anyone that might exist beyond what their five senses can experience. While acknowledging such a disinterest in things beyond for some people, we will not be discussing why those people choose agnosticism or atheism. Those are significant topics (doubt and/or denial of things beyond) that deserve respect and attention beyond what will be offered here. Nor will we pretend to provide any sort of definitive history of humanity's curiosity and experience of the beyond. That kind of ambitious effort has been undertaken by many anthropologists, psychologists, theologians and historians over the centuries, persons far more capable than me. Rather, I want to begin with the assumption that many (most?) people do think about – and seek to know and experience – that which is beyond this world and this life. Then, in subsequent chapters, I want to ask about the events and places and writings and people through whom people have experienced points of connection with the beyond, the absolute, the transcendent, the divine, God.

Often, especially early in the history of humankind, super– natural (i.e. beyond the natural) events/occurrences often caused people to wonder from whence come such extra-ordinary things. Whether thunder and lightning from above or earthquakes below; whether the curse of illness or the blessing of healing; whether seeing an elderly person take their last breath or experiencing a baby take their first, there have always been experiences that pushed people beyond life's ordinary, natural experiences, exacting wonder and awe (positively) or fear and trembling (negatively). Enchantment is a word often used to positively speak about wonder and awe, about things seemingly from beyond that appear magical and mystical. Think of the magical in a baby's first smile or the mystical in a person's love relationship with another person. Superstition is a word often used to describe the beliefs and feelings that arise from fear and anxiety about that which people cannot understand, that is, the unknown which lies beyond their control. Think of the fear and superstition that causes a person to not return to the scene of a bad accident or the anxiety and superstition of bargaining with God about the survival of one's child from a life-threatening illness.

Again, enchantment is a positive response to supernatural events that often elicits wonder and awe; superstition is a more negative response based on fear and anxiety, often accompanied with subsequent efforts to placate or appease whatever transcendent, divine, beyond might have appeared responsible for the curse or judgment. Religious rituals from time immemorial (e.g. worship, prayer, sacrifice and liturgy) can be expressions of gratitude offered by people to their God; other religious rituals (e.g. animal sacrifices and self-mutilation) have been human attempts to appease or bargain with the transcendent, the divine, the beyond, for curses or negative judgments. Prayer is a near universal activity people use to communicate with the beyond for a variety of purposes, positive and negative: expressing gratitude, seeking guidance, invoking blessing, but also when needing consolation, or appealing for help and grasping for aid.

Faith, while at times employed to describe the confidence or trust one person has in another person, more often refers to the attitude and posture one has before God. Saying a person has faith is tantamount to saying they are religious, that is, said person acknowledges and bows before a deity. Faith usually follows a person's encounter – and then connection – with God. Depending on the character, demands and judgement of particular Gods, religious faith takes different forms; faith could involve fear and occasion dreaded obedience, and/or faith might stimulate trust, and perhaps inspire greater self-denial and altruistic service.

A very interesting phenomenon occurred in Western Civilization during the 17th and 18th centuries that relates to our topic of interest: points of connection between humanity and the beyond. This phenomenon, this period in history, is called The Enlightenment or The Age of Reason. It was during this time that people and cultures, especially in Europe, were expanding their knowledge about the world; science and philosophy began to replace superstitious views regarding nature, fundamental convictions about human behavior and traditional religious dogmatism. Humanity appeared to be explaining things – human and worldly – without reference to God, a transcendent being, someone beyond. This advancement (?) in humanity led to an optimism about the future, stimulating greater human confidence in understanding and managing the world.

It was primarily the horrors and devastation of the First World War that called into question just how advanced the world had, in fact, become, and whether science and reason were all they were purported to be. How could such barbarity happen on European soil, where knowledge and human development had reached such an advanced level? Two World Wars and multiple genocides in the Twentieth Century pretty much destroyed human arrogance about just how far humanity had come, and how well people were doing at managing the world. Yet, western civilization could not return to the Dark Ages, where superstition and ignorance reigned. In spite of some glaring evils/curses that occurred concomitantly with this Age of Reason and Enlightenment (brutal warfare and rampant disease), the place of natural explanation and the onset of secularism were here to stay.

Secularism is an interesting term. Defined in the dictionary as 'indifference to or rejection or exclusion of religion and religious considerations' (Merriam-Webster), the actual Latin, 'saeculum,' from which 'secular' comes, means (the present) 'age.' Since religion often focuses on things above and before and beyond, secularism – with its focus on the here and now – came to describe the opposite of the religious. With this minimizing of time and space beyond also came a minimizing, even rejection, of any transcendent One who is beyond, that is, God. If nature and reason could explain most things, what need would there be for God? It was near this time in Christian history (the 19th and early 20th century), that Jesus came to be viewed not so much for his divine, other-worldly, transcendent nature, but as a First century Jewish sage, a teacher and a healer. For many scholars invested in the Enlightenment project, Jesus came to be a great human being; nothing more, nothing less. At this time came The Quest for the Historical Jesus, (Albert Schweitzer, 1906) challenging the Church's deep commitment to Jesus, the God-man, the Nazarene who was 'one in divine substance with the Father' (cf. the Council of Chalcedon, 451 CE) as the Church had confessed for fourteen plus centuries. Further, in the 1960s, a rejection of most things supernatural led to the (short-lived) 'Death of God' movement, expressed by theologians such as Thomas J.J. Altizer, Paul van Buren, William Hamilton and Gabriel Vahanian. These particular individuals drew some of their secular inspiration from people like Anglican Bishop John A.T. Robinson, who quoted the German theologian Dietrich Bonhoeffer. While differing in significant ways with one another, the above names were all seeking to find legitimacy and language for Christian faith in a time when traditional ways of referencing God were being questioned/threatened.

My reason for discussing secularism, following The Age of Reason and Enlightenment, is to show how during this turbulent time in history there was a scrambling to hold-on to the reality and remnants of God, the divine, the religious beyond. For those who wanted to maintain religious faith, in the face of such secular confrontation, just what could one show as a connection point with God. If God, as the Church had confessed, was a reality, and that reality could be known, then what events or places or people or writings could be identified as revealers of that God? Where specifically in history had that God shown-up?

Two examples (only two for purposes of brevity) from the 19th and 20th centuries in Church history may prove helpful for showing the importance of connection points with God or where God was thought to have showed-up: Heilsgeschichte and Neo-Orthodoxy.

Heilsgeschichte ('Salvation History')

This fancy, technical German term in Historical Theology refers to the ways and places God revealed God-self in history through the history of Ancient Israel and the Church. From Moses and the Burning Bush, to Abraham's call, to the Exodus out of Egypt, to the Conquest of the Land, to the words of the prophets and more, the people of Israel laid claim to the conviction that the Almighty God of Creation was actively involved in their Heils (salvation) Geschichte (history). This Heilsgeschichte also included the life, death and resurrection of Jesus and then the Church (i.e. a sort of red thread woven through history, indicating connection points). At these particular times and in these specific places the eternal God from beyond made contact and willed connection with humanity. Education about – and celebration of – these connection points provided ongoing remembrance of God's activity in history. In contrast to a more naturalistic (Deistic/Theistic/liberal) view that the Divine was to be experienced in most every square inch of worldly reality, there now was a concept that affirmed God's connection with the world in particular sacred, salvation events in world history: Heilsgeschichte.

Neo-Orthodoxy (Traditional belief [orthodoxy] with new [neo] urgency)

It was within the context of 20th century European trauma that the theology of Neo-Orthodoxy emerged. As nationalism grew and Christian denominations laid claim to God's favor, there arose a new (neo) form of (orthodox) Christian theology that advocated for a Christianity that could hopefully resist domestication; neither one nation nor one people should claim to hold primacy of place in God's economy. It was the Swiss theologian, Karl Barth, who was initially responsible for this new form of orthodoxy, soon to be joined by theologians such as Emil Brunner and Friederich Gogarten. The resistance these Neo-Orthodox theologians offered was against some of the voices, in Church and society, who were now convinced that God was revealing God-self in the (Nazi) awakening of Germany through its ordained leader, Adolf Hitler. Neo-Orthodox theology put forward that God's final, ultimate and definitive connection point was in the life, death and resurrection of Jesus Christ, related to – yet going beyond – the Covenant of God with Israel. In Barth's attempt to counter Hitler as one more revelation of God in Heilsgeschichte, as affirmed by the Nazified German Christians (the Deutsche Christen), he affirmed Jesus Christ as God's definitive, salvatory (final?) point of connection for all of humanity. While Barth's 'Christ alone' (Solus Christus) theology effectively served to galvanize the protesting Confessing Church (the Bekennende Kirche) against the established Deutsche Christen in the 1930s, it also unfortunately morphed into and encouraged a theology of Christian superiority. What served to resist idolatry in one generation (i.e. affirming Christ, not Hitler, as an authentic point of connection) must be re-examined – so as to prevent hubris and exclusivism – in subsequent generations. But, for our purposes here, Neo– Orthodoxy was one example of (over)emphasizing a single connection point (Anknüpfungspunkt) with God. We dare not be too critical of the faithful Confessing Christians in Germany (fighting for their lives) who were combating the idolization of one (demonic) point of connection (i.e. Adolf Hitler) by hyper-focusing on one other point of connection (i.e. Jesus Christ). In hindsight, one could argue, with Karl Barth, Dietrich Bonhoeffer, and others, that the universal love of the world – and with that all of humanity – in Jesus Christ (i.e. the Church's connection point with God) was certainly closer to the truth than Hitler's exclusive love of only things Aryan/Germanic (i.e. the National Socialist's connection point with a Teutonic God), expressed in Mein Kampf and Nazi propaganda.

So far, the human desire for connection with the beyond, with some attendant rewards and risks in seeking connection. While there will likely be no return to a time before the Enlightenment and Age of Reason and while secularism, with its perennial suspicion regarding things above and beyond human sensory awareness, will always be present, there seems to be good and sufficient evidence that most of humanity (you name the percentage) will continue to inquire about and desire some connection points with God, the beyond. With that in mind, we now turn to examples of events and places that somehow provoke divine connection.

Chapter Two

Events and Places Provoking Divine Connection

It is important to acknowledge, even though it will not be our focus, that from time immemorial humans – historic and pre-historic – have found connections to the transcendent, the divine, within things natural. From thunder and lightning to plants and animals, humans have gotten what they consider to be glimpses of God in the things of nature. Often religious ceremonial traditions were created around the cycles of nature and the cosmos. Think of Stonehenge on Salisbury Plain in Wiltshire, England, from (at least) the fourth century BCE, where religious activity first included cremation and burial and rituals about the afterlife, to the observance of the sunset of the winter solstice and the sunrise of the summer solstice, creating an awareness of what lies beyond. The movement of the huge stones, impossible for mere mortals, was attributed to supernatural forces. The design of the site included a celestial observatory for the prediction of eclipses and the equinox, as these early peoples sought and lived with the awareness of transcendent reality. Religion for ancient peoples was not a separate activity, but built into the fabric of everyday existence: life and sustenance and survival as well as death and the afterlife.

Close to my home is the 'center of the universe' for Dakota natives. Bdo'te (a place where two rivers meet) is where the Mississippi and Minnesota Rivers converge; this geography is – according to Dakota tradition – the place of creation, marked by the Coldwater Spring. Mendota and Mendota Heights both get their names from this convergence near the well-spring where all creation began. There exists a beautiful, yet painful and complex, history related to this area, ranging from its most sacred origins millennia ago, through the creation of a concentration camp for 1,600 Dakota Sioux natives in 1862 near Ft. Snelling to contain 'Indians on their way to removal from Minnesota,' (Governor Alexander Ramsey) to the near desecration of sacred burial lands on Pilot Knob in the late 20th century. A fascinating and tragic history is layered here in my backyard about earlier peoples and their transcendent experiences with land and water and sky. One cannot understand nor appreciate the Dakota People's (to name just one indigenous group) experience without factoring in their assumed beliefs in a divine presence in every square inch of creation. For Indigenous Peoples in America, all of nature contained connection points with the divine, the Great Spirit.

Although there are multiple events and places important in the life of Siddhartha Gautama (the Buddha), we highlight here the traditional place assigned for his 'Enlightenment' at Bodh-gaya under the Bodhi Tree. Having spent a number of years seeking ultimate truth in a variety of aesthetic settings, it was there under that tree that the Buddha finally experienced his event of awakening (connection). There are other places revered by Buddhists that relate to special times in Gautama's life, like Lumbini, Sarnath and Kushinagar, but the Buddha's ultimate connection point with truth, transcendent reality, was under that tree at that time, the 3rd century BCE. What sometimes has kept Buddhism from being seen as a Bonafide world religion, and more resembling a philosophy or way of life pursuing ultimate truth, is that it lacks the more established concept of belief in a divine being, a God. Rather than being grounded in a universal, almighty, divine being, Buddhism seeks a final state of Enlightenment, in which all temporal pain and anxiety and brokenness are gone. Through the discipline of the Eight-fold Noble Path, human beings can strive for release from all worldly attachment, which for them is something resembling the Christian idea of Heaven, but not identical. Nirvana is rather a blessed state of non-being, non-existence, bliss, not just another place and another time. While not identical to a connection point with God, Buddhists do speak of their experience of Enlightenment and awakening as a connection with what is ultimate and absolute. We must remember that no perfect comparison between different religious faiths can be made; a respectful posture is to allow each to define their understanding of the ultimate, not to impose our experience or view on all others. For this reason, while I hope my characterizations of other faiths is accurate, I remain open to correction and learning.

Shifting now to Jews and Judaism, we approach what may be a more familiar notion of humans seeking and experiencing connection with a divine other. Often called the historical beginning of monotheism (belief in One God), Judaism displays a number of events and places of divine connection with the One God of all creation. To read the ancient texts of this people (called the Hebrews, Israel and Jews at different times in their history) is to encounter multiple occasions where they claim to experience the presence (Shekhinah) of Almighty God: Yahweh, Elohim, Jehovah. The calling of Abraham, the sacrifice of Isaac, the great Flood, the Covenant at Sinai, the words of the prophets, the giving of the Land, the return from Exile, the building of the temple and more are understood to be connection points with Yahweh-God. (Reference earlier our description of Heilsgeschichte.) However, in Jewish tradition, it was the Exodus out of Egypt that remains their primal, most important salvation event, followed by the giving of the Law and the establishment of a Covenant on Mt. Sinai. It was there and then that a formal, eternal connection was established by God with Israel, the Jews. (This saving/covenantal experience of Exodus ranks for Jews on a par with the saving/covenantal experience of Christians in the sacrificial death of Jesus on the cross of Calvary.)

From this (Jewish) community of faith came a significant event in the first century CE, within a fairly small geographic area. Although the birth, childhood and vagrancy of its leader (Jesus) caught little attention for thirty years, a final confrontation with the authority of the Romans in Jerusalem resulted in an event that significantly changed the history of the world. It was finally the crucifixion (event) of Jesus of Nazareth on Golgotha's hill in Jerusalem (place) in about 33 CE – and then the community's experience of this Crucified One's resurrected presence –

that sparked a religious movement which displayed a connection point with God that has only recently been rivaled (by Islam) in sheer number of followers. In the life, death and resurrection of Jesus of Nazareth, billions of people – spanning two thousand years – have claimed to experience a connection point with God. The divine vicarious offering of eternal life for all human beings through the death and resurrection of Jesus (i.e. the Church's Master Narrative) remains a remarkable story of a divine connection point that Christian people have believed was orchestrated by God. This vicarious offering of eternal salvation, while not immediately liberating people from all their present pains and oppression, does promise an eternal connection with God that has the potential of transforming the present world as people trust that future.

So far, ancient, native, Jewish and Christian events and places provoking divine connection. Sadly, it took the death of three thousand lives on September 11, 2001, and a Western world set on edge against Islam because of the actions of a few radical Muslims, for many in America to see a need for learning more about this 'other' monotheistic faith. The challenge for many leaders in the Christian Churches was to help the laity understand the difference between authentic, ethical and moral Islam/Muslims and the more violent, hateful beliefs and actions of particular members of radicalized Muslim groups. The media offered little help in protecting this important differentiation, often choosing to amalgamate the terms Islam, radical Muslims and terrorists.

For our purposes here, it is important to discuss the events and places provoking Divine connection in Islam, realizing – as with most every religious tradition – that radicalized, separatists can often give any faith group a bad name. Two examples of pan-Islamist radical groups are al-Qaeda and al-Shabaab; more focused militant groups include Boko Haram based in Nigeria and ISIS in Iraq and Syria. It was in about the year 610 CE, when Muhammad ('peace be upon him' or pbuh), (son of Abdullah ibn Abd al-Muttalib and Amina bint Wahb), who was then forty years old, reported being visited by angel Gabriel in a cave (the place) and there received his first revelation (the event) from God. From that connection point with God, Muhammad went out to preach the Oneness of God (Tawhid) and that the right way of life involves complete submission (slm) to Allah (God). To this day, the birth place of Muhammad (Mecca) is revered, and is close to the place of the Quran's revelation to Muhammad. Also, in Mecca is the al-Ka' bah, believed by Muslims to be the House of God. A very conflicted place in the Mideast is the city of Jerusalem; this singular city is of great importance for Jews, Christians and Muslims. For Jews, pieces of the Second Temple (the Western Wall) completed in 515 BCE remain to this day; for Christians, Jerusalem is the place of Jesus' dedication, his visit at age twelve, his last week, the Last Supper, Jesus' crucifixion and ascension; for Muslims, Muhammad (pbuh) was transported in a Night Journey from Mecca to Jerusalem in 621 CE., and in that single night also visited Heaven. Today, on the famous Temple Mount in Jerusalem stands the great Al-Aqsa Mosque of Islam. So many divine events happened in-and-near this sacred place for three of the world's monotheistic faith traditions that perpetual conflict seems inevitable UNLESS all three come to respect and validate the important connection points with God of the other two.

Obviously, one could enumerate hundreds, if not thousands, of other events and places in the history of humankind that have provoked divine connection. Listing these few is only to give examples of the importance billions of people have found in seeking and honoring – beyond nature – events and places where some kind of experience of God, has been had. Listing these few sets before us a mere smattering of connection points between humanity and some fashion of divinity.

If we can resist the arrogant temptation of elevating our own particular religious connection points with God (events and places) above all others, and to the exclusion of all others, we can grow in an appreciation for the variety and beauty of multiple connection points around us.

Chapter Three

People Seen as Connections with the Beyond

It is important to acknowledge that human intermediaries with the beyond go far back in the history of civilization. From the caveman and cavewoman on, sages and shamans and medicine men have been highly respected and valued members of societies, serving the people as connection points with the divine, as each group understood it. Only in modern times have the priestly classes been (in certain places) demoted from semi-divine persons to more ordinary, secular presences. Such 'called, recognized, and anointed/ordained persons' were – and are – known for their closeness and connection to God, and in those roles performed rites and rituals to keep connection points alive and functioning.

Moses, of Jewish tradition, can be considered one such called, recognized and anointed/ordained person, who lived in the 2nd millennia BCE, known for his leadership in bringing the people of Israel out of bondage in Egypt (@1250 BCE) to Mount Sinai. It was there that he received a divine revelation, and a Covenant was established with Israel's God, their divine partner, Yahweh. The biblical narratives involving Moses are in the books of Exodus and Leviticus. Moses' elder brother, Aaron, actually functioned as Israel's high priest for a period of time, while Moses continued to be respected for his connection to God. The political leadership in Israel passed to the Judges and Saul and David and Solomon down through the years, but we need to remember that key to their leadership was an assumed closeness and their ongoing ability to be connection points with Yahweh, their God. Anointing with oil was a ritual for formally recognizing and empowering these leaders.

Another group of people in the history of Israel that were essential for an active, responsible life of connecting with God was the Hebrew prophets, persons like Isaiah, Jeremiah and Ezekial. Prophets were called and recognized as persons who received and then passed along living words from beyond, from God. Especially called to help the people of Israel stay in tune with and faithful to the covenant relationship established earlier with Abraham and then Moses, the prophets can be understood as connection persons with God, whose vocation was to provide dynamic, living awareness of God for all the people.

Staying with the Jewish tradition a bit longer, we can now look to **Jesus.** In addition to the cross and resurrection events discussed earlier, Jesus' very (Jewish) person, his words and deeds, have also been considered points of connection between people and God. At various times, Jesus has been described as 'prophet, priest and king.' To engage the life and legacy of Jesus is to reflect on his powerful parables and his profound words of wisdom. It is well within Christian tradition to say that followers of Jesus have religiously listened to the scriptural words (of Jesus) expecting to hear a Word from God. The words, deeds, death and resurrection of Jesus are, for Christians, connection points with God.

Approximately six hundred years after Jesus, on the Arabian Peninsula, came **Muhammad** (pbuh). Seen as the founder of another monotheistic world religion (Islam), Muhammad is known as one who was keenly aware of Jewish and Christian tradition but who, seeing ongoing conflict among adherents of those religions, sought a better way, a way closer to authentic connection to God. As mentioned earlier, Muhammad (pbuh) experienced faith and wisdom in a variety of ways before finally receiving what he considered to be God's (Allah) final revelation. In his now famous cave experience, Muhammad (pbuh) received revelation from God through Angel Gabriel, in what is now the Arabic Quran. Muslims consider Muhammad (pbuh) to be God's final prophet, yet very much in line with Moses, Jesus and several others, hence one (the most important) connection point with God. Muslims would consider it idolatry to say that Muhammad was more than human, say divine or Almighty. But, a connection point for sure.

Moving beyond the connection point/persons of the three largest monotheistic world religions, we can also learn from Confucius in China; the Bab, Baha'u' llah and 'Abdu'l-Baha' of the Baha'i tradition; Joseph Smith of the Latter-Day Saints; Sun Myung Moon of the Unification Church, and the Popes/priests/saints of the Roman Catholic Church, to mention only a few.

Confucius (551-479 BCE) is known as a Chinese philosopher/teacher, not a religious guru or founder of a world religion. While some of his followers think of his thoughts and morality along religious lines, most consider him strictly a wise sage who teaches how life is to be lived. Confucius emphasized filial piety and the veneration of ancestors, often repeating the Silver Rule, 'Do not do unto others what you do not want done to yourself.' Sound familiar? I name Confucius here, not because he is a conduit or connection with God (per se) but, because he is looked to by over 6 million people worldwide (just today) as a connection point with ultimate reality and truth. While not a theistic religion, Confucianism is a part of humanity's search for something beyond, and Confucius is the person through whom some connection occurs.

Baha'u' llah (1817-1892 CE) lived in Iran and is the founder of the Baha'i faith, a monotheistic religion that in 2020 registered approximately 9 million adherents world-wide. He believed in the unity of all people and the essential worth of all religions. Two other figures play important roles in the early Baha'i tradition: the Bab (1819-1850 CE) and 'Abdu'l-Baha (1844-1921 CE). While affirming these three primary figures for their Baha'i faith, adherents also acknowledge other manifestations of God in the founders of other major world religions: Buddha, Jesus and Muhammad, for example. Over 9 million people today find a connection point with God through these Baha'i persons.

Joseph Smith (1805-1844 CE) is the undisputed founder of America's largest non-mainline Christian denomination (Mormonism and Latter-day Saints). Living during the Second Great Awakening in Nineteenth Century America, Smith experienced a series of visions. In 1823 CE, he reports an encounter he had with an angel/prophet (Moroni), being instructed to locate a buried book of golden plates inscribed with a Judeo-Christian history of America. The English translation of those plates became the Book of Mormon. Millions of people today are part of the Church of Jesus Christ of Latter-day Saints, and branch denominations of that church. Here it is sufficient to say that Joseph Smith, with the help of the angel Moroni, was and remains, a connection point with God for over 17.5 million people in approximately 32,000 congregations.

Sun Myung Moon (1920-2012 CE) was a Korean religious leader who, with his wife Hak Ja Han, were considered by their followers to be their 'True Parents.' In his Divine Principle book, Moon advocated for an anti-communist unification of North and South Korea, and further global unification under his messianic leadership. He founded the Holy Spirit Association for the Unification of World Christianity in Seoul, South Korea in 1954, and, while boasting about 3 million members worldwide in 2024 (100,000 in the United States), has been considered by many to be a dangerous cult involving mind-control and unlawful business practices. Yet, Sun Myung Moon has been — and still is — regarded by millions of people as a connection point with God.

The **Popes, Bishops, Priests and Saints of the Roman Catholic Church** might not seem, at first glance, like likely candidates for our study of connection points with God. Jesus, and the Bible yes. . . but the Popes, Bishops, priests and saints? We could include all clergy in the Christian tradition, but the Popes, Bishops, priests and saints of the Roman Catholic Church seem to represent more ontological otherness than Protestant pastors. Of course, we are talking in the Roman Catholic tradition about real human beings here, nothing less, yet presumably something more. Of course, we can list standard human qualities like kindness and compassion and generosity; let's complete the list with lust and power and pride and pedophilia. Yes, humans from start to finish. Yet, the ontological otherness in the Roman Catholic Church's clergy has to do with the power conveyed upon ordination: power to forgive sins in the name of Jesus, power to exorcise demons using the Holy Spirit, power to change bread and wine into the body and blood of Jesus during the Eucharist. In fact, more 'something' than other human beings, Popes, Bishops, priests and saints are looked-to as connection points with God. These very human persons are conduits with the beyond. They all join the ranks of sages, shamans, Moses, the prophets, Jesus, Muhammad, Confucius, the Bab, Baha'u' llah, 'Abdu'l-Baha, Joseph Smith and Sun Myung Moon. . . and many, many more through the centuries.

If we resist the arrogant temptation of elevating our own particular religious connection points with God (events, places and people) above all others, and to the exclusion of all others, we can grow in an appreciation for the variety and beauty of multiple connection points around us.

Chapter Four

Writings Given Authority from Beyond

Sacred writings have an intriguing way of taking-on authority from beyond. People can read Shakespeare and Tolstoy and Dostoyevsky and Cervantes hoping to enjoy the inspiration of human authorship and greatness. But, when people lay hold of the Hebrew Torah, the Christian Bible, the Muslim Quran, the Hindu Bhagavad-Gita, the Buddhist Dhammapada, or the Taoist Zhuangzi and Tao Te Ching (for example), they often bring an expectation that something more than human authorship and greatness is involved. Most – not all – people are anticipating a word or a thought from beyond, that is, experiencing a connection point with God, when they engage a sacred text. Granted, such high expectation is most often limited to sacred texts from one's OWN religious tradition. Christians may examine and discuss thoughts in the Muslim Quran, yet anticipation of a word from God would more likely arise when they approach their Bible. Jews may find the four Christian Gospels interesting, but would most likely spend their devotional time with the Torah, the Talmuds or Midrashim of their own tradition.

So just what is it in those sacred texts that motivates some people to think they are from beyond, that is, that they possess an authority that exceeds mere human creativity and wisdom? To ask such serious questions about the divine authority of sacred texts is obviously to move beyond any simple, dogmatic answer like, "Well, they just do!" Here we are asking what it is about those texts that prompts certain individuals/communities to affirm that something more than human wisdom is here involved? To ask why certain people affirm the divine authority of their specific sacred texts is because certain other people do not. There does not appear to be some intrinsic, magnetic force, within any one of those texts, that creates universal acknowledgment of divine authority, otherwise every human being would bow before only that text.

One word related to this question of why persons ascribe divine authority to certain sacred texts is the word 'inspiration.' Literally, this concept means 'God breathed.' While this notion can refer to a motivation within human beings that provokes larger than life thoughts or actions, such as, "She was really inspired to say those profound things and it really moved the audience to do even greater things," the idea of inspiration is most often used to speak about a force for motivation that is greater than mere human emotion and drive. Most often, inspired material refers to thoughts and ideas that come from beyond. Christian people will say that the writers of their Bible were inspired, that is, they were using human words to express deeper, divine thoughts. Muslims believe that the Arabic words that prophet Muhammad (pbuh) heard from angel Gabriel, that were then recorded in the Quran, were inspired in that they came from beyond, that is, they were 'God breathed.'

A second word related to this question of why persons ascribe divine authority to certain sacred texts is the word 'revelation.' Beyond affirming that a text is inspired ('God breathed') and comes from beyond, is to refer to that text as a revelation, meaning that something more about the beyond is shown, displayed, unfolded, revealed. Most religious traditions maintain that their sacred events, places, people and writings are revelations from God; not only did 'God breathe' in those texts, but God also displayed something of God-self in those texts. Inspiration and revelation often go together. Through sacred texts, through revelation and inspiration, connection with God is made.

Now, on to the question of why certain people assign divine authority to their sacred texts, knowing that other people do not. What resides in those texts that draws people in and occasions some to say, "In these very human words I hear something from beyond, I experience the voice of God, and have learned something about the very character of God? I love Shakespeare but, in x, y or z sacred text, I feel that God is speaking to me!" That is what authority from beyond sounds like. Some human beings, Jews in particular, experience a voice from beyond in the words from their Torah, for example Deuteronomy 6:4: "Hear, O Israel: Yahweh is our God, Yahweh is one." Muslims affirm the truth of Allah (God) as merciful, as revealed in their inspired, sacred text, the Quran: Surah 1:1-2, 3:31, 16:7 and 24:20, to name only a few. Christians could easily say God speaks to them from beyond in verses like John 3:16 ("For God so loved the world that he gave his only Son, so that everyone who believes in him may not perish but may have eternal life.") and Romans

1:16 ("For I am not ashamed of the gospel; it is the power of God for salvation to everyone who has faith. . . "). Buddhists, while not hearing the following words from a divinity, a God, would say that such wisdom here in their Dhammapada comes from beyond, from an 'eternal rule:' "Conquer the angry one by not getting angry; conquer the wicked by goodness; conquer the stingy by generosity, and the liar by speaking the truth. Hatred does not cease by hatred, but only by love; this is the eternal rule. Better than a thousand hollow words is one word that brings peace."

So, what resides in sacred texts that draws people in and elicits belief and faith in their transcendent quality, their being 'God breathed?' Allow me to suggest that a connection point with something beyond, is created because of a resonance. Merriam-Webster's dictionary defines resonance as 'a quality of evoking response.' When given (sacred) texts resonate within a person on a deep, transcendent level, that person often assigns to them inspirational value, revelational status and divine origin. The words they are reading provoke a connection with the beyond. In fact, those persons assign those sacred texts authority, as from beyond, insofar as they resonate with existing ideas of divinity, of God. Creating and encouraging experiences of resonance appear to be the way God, the beyond intends things. Human beings are given the opportunity of connecting, but never forced to connect. Likewise, when a person states that 'something' does not foster connection with God and is not a revelation and does not appear inspired, that person is essentially saying that that 'something' does not resonate with their existing thoughts and feelings about God.

If we can resist the arrogant temptation of elevating our own particular religious connection points with God (events, places, people and writings) above all others, and to the exclusion of all others, we can grow in an appreciation for the variety and beauty of multiple connection points around us.

Chapter Five

Human Desire for Perfection in Revelation

There appears to be a correlation between people believing in the perfection of God and then people hoping/believing that certain sacred texts must be perfect because they come from God. It has been asked, "If God has chosen to reveal God's-self in particular words and concepts, why would God not somehow ensure that such words and concepts are pure, infallible and inerrant, just like God?" Further, "If one is to place one's absolute dependence, one's eternal security, on those sacred words, those concepts, those promises, they darn well better be true and accurate." And, "If certain words or concepts in our sacred text appear to be absolutely true and others less absolute, how are we supposed to know which to trust and which to reject?" There appears to be a human desire in most – not all – people to have perfection in revelation, in their sacred texts, because so much is at stake. We are not here dealing with the color of paint we choose for our family room or the locations we are considering for our summer vacation or the brand of car that gives us the best mileage. When dealing with our religious texts, as revelations of God from beyond, we believe we are dealing with pretty important stuff. Does not our existence, our hope and our future involve a proper understanding of the will and the ways of God, as brought to us in sacred texts? And so, the human desire for perfection in revelation is completely understandable, yet is equally unreal in its expectation.

While the Christian Bible has always possessed an authority greater than mere literature, it is only in the last couple of centuries that the ideas of 'inerrancy' and 'infallibility' regarding biblical texts have appeared and, for many Christians, taken-on a near absolute value. Mostly in response to the Age of Reason – the Enlightenment – have some schools and denominations in more conservative Protestant Churches encouraged a more absolute and unassailable understanding of their scriptures. With the academic disciplines of biblical and historical study (especially in the 19th and 20th centuries), more openly investigating and critiquing the scriptures for greater clarity and authenticity, came certain parts of the Church community feeling a need to dig their heals in deeper to guard their sacred scriptures from attack and erosion. Hence, the proposals that sacred scripture was – by divine decree – inerrant in historical detail and infallible in theology. Today, it is the conservative and fundamentalist denominations (or non– denominations) that proclaim most loudly these unrealistic 'safeguards,' in preaching and teaching. For these groups, defending the absolute, inerrant, infallible status of the Bible is tantamount to defending God.

More liberal and progressive (mainline) Christian denominations have welcomed the fruits of 'Higher Critical' methods of biblical interpretation, believing that God can speak even through the broken, imperfect words and concepts of human texts. It is important to say here that some of the more conservative biblical interpreters and traditions have differentiated between 'Higher' and 'Lower' Biblical interpretation (criticism). This means understanding that some (erroneous) historical and geographical detail in the bible is a reflection of the world view from that time. For example, Lower Biblical criticism understands that the Ptolemaic view of the physical universe in the First century has been rightly updated by a Copernican worldview after the Enlightenment. These same conservative interpreters usually reject Higher Biblical criticism that might propose, for example, that Jesus' resurrected presence was a sort of emotional/psychological experience for the disciples, not a physical presence of a dead man. This conflict over biblical interpretation – conservative or progressive – continues to the present day. Both groups speak of the importance and inspiration of sacred scripture; the difference is over how that importance and inspiration is understood.

The human desire for perfection in revelation is at the heart of the above controversy. Whereas, some Christian people require/need biblical inerrancy/infallibility for their faith to have a solid foundation and a reliable connection point, other Christian people appear to be comfortable with an inspired scripture that includes historical error and even theological contradiction.

Moving on to perfection in revelation in the Islamic Quran, we find similarities and differences with some Christian understanding. I believe it is correct to say that Muslims understand the (Arabic) Quran to accurately express – and infallibly convey – what God (Allah) intended for humanity to receive in the revelation to Muhammad (pbuh) through the angel Gabriel. Muslims accept that when the Quran is translated into other languages it perhaps involves human interpretive errors not intended by Allah. However, in the original Arabic, which has been accurately transmitted down through fifteen centuries, there exists no error, nor includes any human interpretation. This more absolute understanding bears some resemblance to a conservative Christian view involving inerrancy and infallibility. When Muslims or conservative Christians are asked about the human element in the transmission of God's revelation to humanity that comes, for example, through Muhammad (pbuh) or the Gospel writers, the answer often is, "Somehow, God has insured that even through fallible human thoughts and speech and grammar and syntax, God's absolute, perfect Word is preserved in the text." These Christians believe the Holy Spirit insures such perfection in revelation. These Muslims believe that the angel Gabriel's utterances are divinely insured, and transcribed in Arabic.

The above convictions, regarding the infallibility and inerrancy of sacred texts, are ultimately faith declarations, because any scientific proof involving divine activity lies outside the capacity for human beings to confirm when using their five senses. While proving the perfect, absolute, supernatural source behind any sacred text is impossible, it can be said that (some) human beings clearly desire (need?) perfection in revelation because they seek connection with that which is perfect, that which is beyond, and any imperfect connection risks a faulty relationship.

Moving beyond the desire for perfection in sacred texts, there is a similar desire (need?) for perfection in the Christian elevation of Jesus from merely a good Jewish person living in the first century CE. to his being the only, truly divine son of God. And, if Jesus is the divine son of God (who is perfect by definition), then he (Jesus) clearly must be without sin. As Christian tradition has it, Jesus is the final perfect sacrifice for the forgiveness of sins and the salvation of the world. Other earlier sacrifices for sin (animals in particular) were blemished and imperfect, but Jesus, now the perfect and final sacrifice, must be without sin.

Progressive Christians appear not to need a sinless Jesus, because a pure sacrificial element (in Jesus' life, death and resurrection) is not so important. They would say that God was revealed in Jesus' life but that imperfections, like in the Bible, don't invalidate God's revelation through it. Jesus' life – because he's human – no doubt included some things sinful; but God can and does still speak through him.

Roman catholic tradition and theology have pushed the perfection of Jesus even further up the genetic scale by holding that the mother of Jesus, Mary, must also be perfect and without sin for her son to be sinless and pure. And then, further, even to the immaculate conception of Mary. So, how far up the family tree must one go? At the base of all these efforts at perfection is the human desire that any revelation of God must share in the perfection of God's-self. I refer to these efforts in the Christian community that seek perfection as conservative, even fundamentalist, because progressive Christianity does not seem to need, nor demand, such perfectionist criteria for revelation. Stated directly, progressive Christian theology would say that God is able to – in fact, God must – use imperfect vessels for revelation, because that's all God has to work with. Whether the imperfect person of Moses or the duplicitous lives of the prophets or the fully human life of Jesus or the conflicting narratives of the Gospels or the brokenness in the lives of Popes and bishops and pastors, down to the imperfect and struggling people God uses to carry-out God's work, revelation can and does happen in broken ways, in spite of human desires for more absolute, secure, perfect, infallible, inerrant words and actions. Revelation – connection points – need not be perfect and pure to be authentic and from God.

It has been my observation that Jewish tradition leans into the reality of God's spirit for empowering God's revelation more than either Christian or Muslim tradition. Yes, they would call the Torah and the Prophets and the Writings (the TANAK) sacred; no, they would not call those scriptures infallible nor are they inerrant. For Jews, the communication of God with humanity, if we want to call it that, happens when humans engage the texts in living dialogue within the community of faith. God's spirit (ru'ach), of course, is in the neighborhood, ever breathing life into life, always present when God's people gather and spar about the texts. And, rather than there being just one truth or fact or insight in the text being studied, for Jews, the ancient texts become grist for the mill and a focus for discovering contemporary meaning. There is no intrinsic, 'God meaning', residing in the words or phrases in a text; the meaning is unfolded in the sacred interaction of people with the text. This process or exercise is called midrash, an exposition resulting from human insight, discussion, and even disagreement! The words of the text only take on life in the interaction of people with the text. The texts printed on the page, whether in Hebrew or English or Arabic, are dead letters/words ever waiting to have life breathed into them.

Human beings appear to generally prefer the assurance that certain events, certain places, certain people, and certain writings are divinely pure and perfect, like the God they assume sent them. Things would be so much more locked-down and secure if only these revelatory texts were intrinsically perfect and inerrant, avoiding the human need to invest them with meaning. And, some people think just that. But, for others such a human desire does not account for the challenge God appears to place before humanity: "Trust the faith I have invited you to have in me, search through the broken, yet blessed, experiences and wisdom of the sages in the pages of your sacred scripture, all to hear my living voice. And, do it together" (Yahweh, God, Allah). Connection points are always humanly imperfect, yet are gifts from beyond. They are human events, places, people and writings through whom God can reveal God's-self, should people be humble, open and ready. (The above quote, attributed to God, was written by me. I felt inspired to write those words because those ideas resonate with the God I know in Jesus Christ, the Torah and the Quran. You, the reader, can now decide if those ideas sound like God . . . to you!)

Chapter Six

Idolatry as Understandable, yet Wrong

A close cousin to 'humans desiring perfection in revelation' is the human proclivity towards idolatry, defined in Merriam Webster as 'the worship of a physical object.' If someone has an exceptionally strong attraction to something or someone, we might say they almost idolize it/them. Idolizing is something most people prefer to NOT say about themselves, since most know that humans are to worship God only, not things or people. In the realm of religion, idolatry is an understandable proclivity, because the events, places, people and writings that provide connection with God often take on a mystical quality akin to the beyond itself. While reading about the peace of God in a sacred text, one might actually feel God's peace. Further, if persons assign divine perfection to a connection point, then it's a close step to consider the connection point divine, like the God to whom it points.

Another way of describing something or someone idolized is that it/he/she is simply beyond anything else that person has ever experienced. If one person, for example, has virtually transformed the way another person thinks or behaves, there exists a temptation in the transformed one to idolize/worship that person. If a particular book has given someone a completely new orientation toward life, that person might almost worship that book, or the author. Or, for the one who recently won the state lottery or was given an incredible promotion, such a person might want to idolize the place or person who made such a thing possible. An amplification of normal experience can create a larger-than— life response; idolatry is an understandable human activity.

Let us look at a few examples of idolatry that indicate both why idolatry is understandable and why idolatry is finally unfaithful, often unhelpful and thus declared wrong. First, let us reference the Hebrew scriptures where Israel is chastised for idolizing and worshipping a Golden Calf. In Exodus 32, that recounts the people waiting for Moses to return from meeting God on Mt. Sinai, we read about the creation of a gold statue of a calf that could be worshipped. This creation of an idol was the result of the people's impatience with Moses, who was delayed in bringing back his experience with Yahweh G-d. In the prolonged absence of their anticipated connection point (i.e. Moses' word from God), the people clamored for some kind of connection point, tasking Aaron with the creation of an idol. Of course, the text reminds us that God is displeased with their impatience and lack of trust, and hence, God punishes the people for their false worship. Yes, the people's unmet need for – and then creation of – a connection point is understandable. No, just any ole substitute for God won't suffice. The Golden Calf in Exodus 32 is an example of a physical, concrete object being idolized/worshipped; there are many, many such physical objects down through the ages that attempted to create connection points with the beyond. Remember the statues on the Easter Islands or the rocks at

Stonehenge. The quest for the Absolute beyond is understandable; yet, concrete idolization is unfaithful, often unhelpful, and thus declared wrong. Most religious traditions say: 'Let only God be God!'

Second, Muslims need to be careful to not idolize the Arabic Quran or the Ka'bah, given the required, elevated respect they have for that text and that Black Cube in Mecca. For sure, the Quran and the Ka'bah are highly regarded and do serve as connection points with Allah – God. Yet, Muslims are taught that those connection points are not equal to Allah, never to be worshipped. Because, if a person assigns perfection or divinity – not simple high regard – to any physical object or person, that individual commits idolatry.

Third, some Christians run the risk of idolatry when calling the Bible the Word of God or thinking that the bread and wine of communion are the very Body and Blood of Christ. Such assignment of (near) divinity to something physical (a human book or bread and wine) is completely understandable, yet deserves our critique. Why? Because, when a person assigns perfection or divinity – not simple high regard – to any physical object or person, that individual commits idolatry. For Christians to avoid idolatry regarding the Bible, they could say, "The Bible is composed of the words of people, yet words that can be used by God." There is a fine line between saying "The words of the Bible are spoken by God to me," and "In the (human) words of the Bible I experience God speaking to me." Similarly, for Christians to avoid idolatry regarding the elements of Holy Communion – bread and wine – they only need to remember what they were taught in catechism or confirmation classes: ". . . in, with and under the bread and wine is Christ's real and living presence." Still bread and still wine, but 'accompanied' by Christ's living presence, gratefully received as a reminder of the forgiveness of God. "In, with and under," much like the love a person receives from another person "in, with and under" a physical gift on their birthday. The gift isn't the love or the person giving it; the love 'accompanies' the physical object. So, with the Bible and the sacraments; connection points with God, but never to be idolized as if they are God.

Fourth, remember the acclamation of divinity for the Führer in Nazi Germany? The people there desired an absolute, divine – yet human – connection point (person) to orchestrate recovery and renewal after World War I, to overcome their despair and disintegration as a people. Very understandable, given the desperate conditions of post-war, depression-era Germany. However, choosing a human idol, with all the risks of narcissism and hubris, believing that such a person was somehow equated with the divine essence, was neither faithful nor helpful. As we saw during the Third Reich, the idolization of Adolf Hitler nurtured an absolute obedience that properly belongs only to God. In that leader's name – and with the absolute obedience of millions of adherents – some of the most inhumane activities known to humankind were unleashed. Whenever anyone assigns perfection or divinity – not simple high regard – to any physical object or person, that individual commits idolatry.

We finally arrive now at perhaps the most problematic example of idolatry for Christians: Jesus, of Nazareth. Jesus was elevated, following his death on a cross and his resurrected presence among some followers, from being a peasant in First century Palestine to being the Christ of God, who is 'co-equal and consubstantial with the Father. . . (and) who is worshipped and glorified' in Christian worship. To question or critique this worship of Jesus is, of course, anathema within Christian tradition; Jesus' divine origin and character is a fundamental tenant of all orthodox Christian belief. One could easily say that the center of Christian reality, like the reason for its global success over two millennia, is the fact that the person who is front and center is not only human, but divine, in origin and character. The very appeal of Christianity is related to the God— man who lies at its beginning. Take away the divine 'essence and substance' of Jesus (Chalcedon 451 CE), who is 'co-equal and consubstantial with the Father'. . . (and) who is worshipped and glorified' (Nicaea 325 CE), and one has gutted the Christian faith of its core, its essence, its unique appeal. This unique appeal, the 'Word became flesh and dwelt among us.' (John 1:14) – the Incarnation – is the core of the Christian tradition's proclamation. Remove this confession, and label the Incarnation of God as idolatry, and one has literally robbed the Christian faith of its historic essence and ultimate appeal to humanity. Would not Christianity then become simply one more expression of religion on the buffet table of humanity's quest for the beyond? Is not the powerful and perennial appeal of Christianity the 'fact' that, in Jesus, we have not only a worldly connection point with God, but that the very being, essence, and substance of the Almighty, Omnipotent, Omniscient, Omnipresent Divine resided in that single, beautiful human being, son of Mary (and Joseph?) in First century Palestine? Perhaps Christianity is one big exception to the prohibition against idolatry? For sure, idolatry (the worship of a physical object or person) is wrong and our worship is to be directed solely to God, the true beyond. Yet, in Jesus – and only Jesus – the prohibition against idolatry would appear to be superseded. That seems to be the Christian claim, the Christian confession, the orthodox position for two thousand years. The appeal and resilience of Christianity as described above ('the Word became flesh') is what makes it attractive. Is the worship of one particular human being (Jesus), in fact, idolatry? I guess we all must decide.

We have looked at several examples of idolatry and how idolatry is quite understandable, yet clearly unfaithful, often unhelpful and thus declared wrong. We've discussed here how idolization of something worldly (e.g. a Golden Calf, an Arabic book or cube, a Christian Bible, a political leader and a human Jesus) is often the result of people, who legitimately seek connection points with God, transforming the connection point with God into a physical piece of God. Idolatry is a very understandable, human activity, yet, an activity wrought with significant danger, hence declared wrong.

Chapter Seven

Pluralism as Multiple Experiences of Connection

We begin here with a working definition of 'pluralism: "a theory that there are more than one or two kinds of (whatever). . ." Specifically, for our topic, pluralism refers to multiple views or beliefs about ultimate reality or the beyond, therefore, multiple points of connection. When we say that some people in our country are Christians and some are Jews and some are Muslims, etc., we are describing America as religiously pluralistic. This reality – religious pluralism – is seen by some people as a positive, good thing, and by others as a negative, bad thing.

Those people – or faith groups – that view religious pluralism as a good thing usually base their conviction on the idea that, while God is One (still monotheism), human beings and communities experience that beyond in many different ways. Rather than seeing such diversity and variety in beliefs as bad, or as a problem, these persons understand their particular faith or belief (system) as one among many, one in a world of great plurality, one color in a rainbow that – when seen altogether – is a beautiful thing.

Religious pluralism, positively understood, chooses to see the reality of God refracted throughout humanity, producing a multitude of colors, of religions, all of which have their origin in that One beyond. For those understanding pluralism as an aberrant or erroneous view of reality, 'beauty' would not be their adjective of choice.

Those people – or faith groups – that view religious pluralism as a bad thing usually base their conviction on the idea that, since truth and ultimate reality and the beyond are One, (which is the basis of monotheism, i.e. belief in One God), then by implication, there ought to be just one proper faith or belief system. Isn't it interesting that those same persons or faith groups understand their faith and belief system to be the correct one! Because of this (usually passionate) faith and belief, even while recognizing other faiths as sincere approaches to the beyond, those others cannot be true, since – by implication – there is just ONE God and ONE belief system. One group of people passionately rejecting religious pluralism would be fundamentalists. Not only do these people focus on the fundamentals of their faith, usually resisting anything interpretive or progressive, these people also hold firmly to the conviction that their fundamental beliefs are the only correct ones. For this reason, an openness to other beliefs about the beyond is, de facto, rejected. To these people, there are not several or multiple connection points with the beyond, but only one connection point. . . theirs! For fundamentalist Christians, that connection point is Jesus, Jesus, only Jesus.

Returning to our theme of connection points with God, it is important to remember that one need not sacrifice belief in One God (monotheism) to affirm that there exist many (a plurality of) views and perspectives about that One God. Muhammad, in the 7th century CE, observed the conflicts between waring Jews and Christians and concluded that they (both monotheistic believers) were all missing something important in worship and obedience. Hence, in the blessed Qu'ran, Muhammad (pbuh) brings to his people an additional revelation, a somewhat amplified perspective about God's peaceful plan and unity of purpose. As any Muslim will tell you, the Qu'ran does not propose another deity, another beyond, another God. Rather, the Qu'ran offers some corrective thoughts, some additional wisdom to earlier, truthful revelations in the Hebrew and Christian scriptures. In fact, the Qu'ran explicitly states that it correctly understands those earlier revelations, it does not contradict them. If anything, it is the Christian scriptures, not the Torah or Qu'ran, that – in places – speaks exclusively and in a manner of supersession over earlier revelations. (See the New Testament book of Hebrews)

Whether in Judaism, Christianity or Islam, there is evidence a plenty within each tradition to support a positive view of pluralism with regard to religious belief. Jews have historically understood themselves to be chosen by G-d for a particular mission: witnessing to the entire world about the grace, mercy and judgement of G-d. Yet, Yahweh God loves and relates to all of humanity. Muslims have historically understood themselves to be recipients and conduits of Allah's will and ways in the world, recognizing that all people, of multiple religious expressions, can and have experienced God's truth. Christians have, unfortunately, as I see it, understood themselves to be the primary, if not sole, custodian of God's Word and ways in the world. For sure, not all Christians – but most – have been taught, and then chose, to believe that there were many religions that think they observe truthful revelations (connections) of God, but only in Jesus of Nazareth does humanity encounter and experience finally the One true God. There have been precious few exceptions down through history (mostly since the Vatican II Council of the Roman Catholic Church in 1965) when Christians affirmed that there are multiple connection points with God. Still today, there is a significant divide in the Christian Church between those who believe that "No one comes to the Father, except through me (Jesus)" (John 14:6) and those who embrace a more pluralistic theology. While not perfect descriptors, the two sides can be labeled 'conservative' and 'progressive.' Progressive Christians have been open to a more pluralistic, comparative theology. The growth of conservative churches and denominations would suggest that pluralism (that is, that the Church of Jesus Christ is one of many groups having a connection point with God) is not winning the day. Apparently, a more tribal, exclusivist type of religion is preferred over a more global, inclusivist one.

In reality, pluralism, as multiple experiences of connection, is a rather late development in the history of humankind. Across many ethnicities and many varieties of governing systems and many religions throughout history, conflict and warfare have been more often than not the ways these various entities interacted. Competition over geography or resources or governance or gods has been founded on the conviction that one people or place or perspective (ours usually ☺) is the best – if not the only – one ordained by God. Whether a fiefdom in the Middle Ages, or a territory in the modern world such as Prussia, or the oil fields of Saudi Arabia, or the Christian Nationalism of America in 2025, humanity has most often descended to more tribal levels of exclusivity, rather than ascend to the higher plains of inclusivity. Apparently, viewing the 'other' as threat and enemy is preferred to seeing them as neighbor and friend.

Pluralism, in all its expressions, should be less a threat to be resisted – an enemy to be attacked – and more a neighbor to be embraced and a friend to be trusted. Whether a neighbor next door or an adjacent country, pluralism can either be a reality to be simply tolerated or a gift to be celebrated. Religion should be the impetus, the stimulus for connection points between all others, because it has first experienced the (multiple) connection points with YHWH, God, Allah, et. al.

Chapter Eight

The Rewards of Recognizing Multiple Connections

The United States, in 2025, is facing an identity crisis. It can be argued that the present polarity, the cultural battle for the soul of America, is being fought over the very issue of pluralism. Most of the issues that America is facing can be understood as conflicts over beliefs and attitudes regarding race, gender, sexuality, nationality, economics and/or religion. While a complete understanding of our current situation is beyond the scope of this small book, it does seem obvious that a dominant white, male–led, heterosexual, Christian culture, that was assumed for the first two hundred years of our nation's history, will no longer be the dominant demographic of our future. America IS racially very diverse, no longer male controlled, neither sexually defined in a binary fashion, nor only Christian by way of religion. Although there is currently a passionate conflict over these traditional markers, it is not likely that we – as a country – will be returning to the days of yesteryear. Now this evolution (or devolution, depending on one's perspective) of thought and identity can be seen as a threat to be eliminated, a situation to be simply tolerated or – dare I suggest – a blessing to be celebrated. Too much change in too short a time can be overwhelming and even paralyze a people. These four major areas of transition have all evolved significantly in less than a century. Historically speaking, that is a very short time; hence, rebellion in the streets and resistance in the pews. One hears regularly just how threatening the progressive, liberal, WOKE agenda is for many Americans. While we can't slow it down (much), we need to be aware and sensitive just how disturbing and disruptive this amount of change is in such a short period of time.

While discussing pluralism objectively on a head level has its place in academia, it is important to describe the beauty and blessing of this more recent reality in our ordinary, lived experience. Personally, as I have been open to our wide world of differences, our communities marked by diversity, the beauty and blessing of pluralism has served to reduce my fears and lessen my anxiety. Whether acknowledged or not, people who have little exposure to persons who are 'different' do appear to possess some degree of fear. The unknown is precisely that: unknown. And, until encountered and enjoyed, the unknown remains somewhat a threat. I have found no solution to this problem or remedy to this ailment – fear and anxiety – except through taking a risk and stepping forward to meet one's neighbor.

Pluralism, in all of the above ways, can be an opportunity to be embraced. And, religion could be a positive place of affirming a variety of connection points with God and such affirming could lead one to a beautiful world with all kinds of connection points with others. Difference isn't bad; difference is just different! Otherness need not be a threat; otherness is just other! The way we always did things isn't bad; it's just the way we did things! Pluralism values multiple connection points with God and others. Can we embrace pluralism as a gift, as a new approach, for preserving and honoring our world and the God who created it? The alternative, of course, is destroying and dishonoring the world and the God who created it. The choice is ours.

Afterword

I chose the title 'Connection Points with God' because my life has been blessed with an ever-increasing experience of connection with God in multiple other events, places, people and writings.

Let me here summarize my thoughts about connection points with God, my journey, my growth, my conclusions (so far). I join the human family — all of the family in all its shapes and all its marvelous configurations — in desiring a connection with God. I have no master key for knowing — nor any inside track for finding — what was before I came into being nor what is to come when I close my eyes for the last time here. Together, with most of humanity, I desire to know about what was before and after so that I am better able to live responsibly and joyfully in the here and now. Recognizing that we (almost) all desire, on some level, to know what lies beneath and beyond the earth and the sky, it is only a matter of where we entered life and what shaped us in life that dictates what and how and why we inquire of God the way we do. I was born a Caucasian, heterosexual, male, into a middle-class American Christian home. You could write the script. I was grateful that my environment and education prompted me to learn who I was — and was not — and how that environment and education affected my perceptions and priorities. My parents and Lutheran congregation encouraged me to worship God and serve my neighbor.

The events and places that provoked connection points with God for me were largely religious. Sunday School began at age five; confirmation instruction took place in grades 7, 8 and 9; Youth for Christ included me during my high school years; college brought me to a Lutheran institution for higher education; seminary prepared me for Christian ministry as a vocation; graduate study broadened my horizons, etc. etc. Our Savior's Lutheran Church on Southern Avenue in Muskegon, Michigan, was a place of connection with God and other people. Regular worship and religious education there nurtured me in faith and curiosity. At Concordia College in Moorhead, Minnesota, I further absorbed the warmth of Christian community and practiced deeper reflection on things beyond. At Luther Theological Seminary in St. Paul, Minnesota, I expanded my inquiry and was fully indoctrinated into the mainstream Lutheran expression of Christianity. From there parish ministry took me to Moorhead and Brooklyn Park and Afton and Apple Valley. Along the way I ventured beyond Minnesota to places like Germany, Israel, South Africa and Auschwitz, from Muskegon, Michigan, to Davenport, North Dakota, to St. Paul, Minnesota, to Los Angeles, to Phoenix and Tampa and Ft. Lauderdale and New York City. So many places and so many events and experiences: college, seminary, the American Academy of Religion, The International Bonhoeffer Society, the Scholars' Conference on the Holocaust and the Churches, Yad Vashem in Jerusalem, The ELCA Consultative Panel for Lutheran Jewish Relations, the St. Paul Interfaith Network, the Minnesota Multifaith Network, and World Without Genocide. My life has been incredibly full, with a plethora of events and places provoking divine connection.

The people and writings that provoked connection points with God for me were also largely religious. My mother's cousin's husband, George Deery, was extremely important in my early years; George was a steady, supportive kind of 'uncle' that provided security and balance in my mildly insecure and imbalanced family. . . and it was George who invited me to sing in the church choir. I sensed he was connected to God, and that inspired me and mentored my connecting.

Pastor Larry Pratt, serving Our Savior's from 1966-70, impressed me as a religious person I respected and wished to emulate. Larry not only appeared connected to God; he inspired me to connect with God in the struggle of race relations in the 1960s.

Professor Paul Sponheim at Concordia College took religion for me from personal to professional, from heart to head, from faith to theology. His intellect was keen and his passion was intense. He helped connect me with the world of theology and philosophy, as did his teacher and mine, Kierkegaard scholar, Reidar Thomte.

Professor James Burness at Luther Theological Seminary was the person responsible for moving my initial interest in Dietrich Bonhoeffer to what would become a life-long preoccupation and passion. His introductory course to Bonhoeffer, in the Fall of 1971, inspired me for eventual involvement and leadership in the International Bonhoeffer Society that continues to this day. The connection to Bonhoeffer – and Bonhoeffer's family in Germany that I came to know very personally –

has been, like for Jim Burtness, an important connection point for faith.

My list of other people who lived connection points with God is really endless. As my earlier book, 50 Shapes of Grace, shows, many people in my life have been life-giving channels of God's goodness and grace.

Writings that have been connections with God likely number in the hundreds. Most would expect that for me, a pastor/theologian, the Bible would rank first regarding divine connection; that is true. For me, that has meant a career-long love affair with the (Greek) New Testament and the (Hebrew) Old Testament. When preparing weekly sermons, the Nestle Greek text was always consulted, and the Hebrew Bible often. Further, as a Lutheran pastor, the sermons, writings and theology of Martin Luther were regular connectors. During the last two decades, the Qu'ran has become a new, best friend, as well. Unfortunately, I am dependent on the English translations of the Qu'ran since I do not read Arabic. The most important – and regular – authors whose writings I visited in fifty years of ministry and theology (beyond the Bible and Martin Luther) and who count for me as connection points with God would be Dietrich Bonhoeffer, Søren Kierkegaard, Paul Tillich, Fyodor Dostoevsky, Jürgen Moltmann, Reinhold Niebuhr, Edward Schillebeekx, James Dunn, Emil Fackenheim and Abraham Joshua Heschel.

Events, places, people and writings were where I made most significant connection with God. The wider my world became, the more diverse were the events, places, people and writings where I saw divine connections. I share my journey of connections in the hope that my connections might creatively evoke similar remembrances and reflections for each reader. It is obvious that my journey did not include the mystical and meditative elements that are practiced in the monastery and the ashram, places of significant connection points for many people. I am a product of Western Christendom that came from Norway, earlier from the University of Wittenburg (Martin Luther), and before that, the Holy See in Rome. Experiencing the divine and expressing the beyond in this way has been my life vocation, for which I am eternally grateful and everyday joyful!

About the Author

John W. Matthews is a retired ELCA Lutheran pastor and adjunct instructor of religion at Augsburg University (Minneapolis). He is a graduate of Concordia College in Moorhead, Minnesota (1971), Luther Theological Seminary in St. Paul, Minnesota (M.Div. 1975 and M.Th. 1982), doing further graduate study at The International Center for Holocaust Education, Yad Vashem, in Jerusalem. His interest in Holocaust studies evolved from his graduate work on the theological legacy of Dietrich Bonhoeffer; he served as President of the International Bonhoeffer Society – English Language Section (2005-2010) and has publish two books on Bonhoeffer. John was a founding member of the ELCA's Consultative Panel on Lutheran–Jewish Relations, serving from 1990-2000. He was one of the authors of 'A Declaration of the Evangelical Lutheran Church in America to the Jewish Community,' (1994) that now hangs in the United States Holocaust Memorial Museum in Washington, DC. John and his wife, Patty, live in Apple Valley, Minnesota, and have five children and eleven grandchildren.